SCHOLASTIC
News
Nonfiction Readers®

Let's Talk Tae Kwon Do

by Laine Falk

Children's Press®
An Imprint of Scholastic Inc.
New York Toronto London Auckland Sydney
Mexico City New Delhi Hong Kong
Danbury, Connecticut

These content vocabulary word builders are for grades 1–2.

Subject Consultant: Thomas Sawyer, EdD, Professor of Recreation and Sport Management, Indiana State University

Reading Consultant: Cecilia Minden-Cupp, PhD, Reading Specialist and Author, Chapel Hill, North Carolina

Photographs © 2009: Alamy Images: 23 top left, 23 bottom left (Aflo Foto Agency), 5 top right, 8 (Inmagine), cover (JupiterImages/Thinkstock); AP Images/Manu Fernandez: 19; Corbis Images: 5 bottom left, 18 (Susana Vera/Reuters), 1, 11 (Hang Xingwei/Xiunhua Press); DK Images/Andy Crawford: 4 top, 12; Courtesy of East Coast Tae Kwon Do Academy, Australia/Sharon Novilla: 4 bottom left, 5 top left, 6; Getty Images: 15 (Allsport Concepts), 13 (Peter Cade); Gotham Taekwon-Do, New York, NY/www.nyct-kd.com: back cover, 2, 5 bottom right, 7, 14; iStockphoto: 21 (Martijn Mulder), 17 top (Andrey Ushakov); PhotoEdit/Tony Freeman: 9; Reuters/You Sung-ho: 17 bottom; VEER: 20 right (Alloy Photography), 4 bottom right, 10 (Digital Vision Photography), 23 bottom right (image 100 Photography), 23 top right (Photodisc Photography), 20 left (Stockbyte Photography), Map 7: Jim McMahon.

Series Design: Simonsays Design!
Book Production: Scholastic Classroom Magazines

Library of Congress Cataloging-in-Publication Data

Falk, Laine, 1974–
Let's talk tae kwon do / Laine Falk.
    p. cm.—(Scholastic news nonfiction readers)
Includes bibliographical references and index.
ISBN-13: 978-0-531-13828-1 (lib. bdg.) 978-0-531-20428-3 (pbk.)
ISBN-10: 0-531-13828-3 (lib. bdg.) 0-531-20428-6 (pbk.)
1. Tae kwon do—Juvenile literature. I. Title.
GV1114.9.F35 2008
796.815'3—dc22   2007042015

No part of this publication may be reproduced in whole or in part, or stored in a retrieval system, or transmitted in any form or by any means, electronic, mechanical, photocopying, recording, or otherwise, without written permission of the publisher. For information regarding permission, write to Scholastic Inc., 557 Broadway, New York, NY 10012.

©2009 Scholastic Inc.
All rights reserved. Published in 2009 by Children's Press, an imprint of Scholastic Inc.
Published simultaneously in Canada. Printed in China.
SCHOLASTIC, CHILDREN'S PRESS, and associated logos are trademarks and/or registered trademarks of Scholastic Inc.
8 9 10 R 18 17 16 15   62

CONTENTS

WORD HUNT

Look for these words as you read. They will be in **bold**.

block
(blok)

instructor
(in-**struhk**-tuhr)

kick
(kik)

bow
(bou)

gi
(gee)

medal
(**med**-uhl)

spar
(spar)

5

Time to Line Up!

A tae kwon do (ty kwon doh) class is about to start.

To begin the class, we **bow** to the **instructor**. What else do we do in our tae kwon do class?

bow

instructor

Tae kwon do is a sport that began in the country of **Korea** (koh-**ree**-uh).

Area of map

Asia

U.S.

Pacific Ocean

CHINA

NORTH KOREA

Pyongyang

EQUATOR

Seoul

N W E S

SOUTH KOREA

JAPAN

We stretch to warm up our bodies.

We wear a uniform called a **gi**. It fits loosely. This makes it easier for us to move around.

gi

Next, we practice how to **kick**. We kick high in the air. We have to learn how to stand on one leg.

kick

The bigger kids stand in front. We watch them and our instructor.

We also practice punches. We learn how to **block**, too. A block is a way to protect your body from a kick or a punch.

block

"Aya!" Sometimes we shout as we practice our punches and kicks.

Later, we **spar**. Sparring is pretend or practice fighting. One person blocks a kick. Another throws a punch!

spar

People try not to hurt each other when they spar. They wear helmets and pads to keep from getting hurt.

Some people in our school can even break bricks and boards! They use their hands and feet. It takes many years of practice to learn how to do this.

People learn to break bricks and boards without hurting themselves.

Sometimes we show off our moves at a match. Winners get a **medal** or trophy. Then, we go back to class to practice some more!

medal

In a match, kicks and punches are worth points. The person with the most points wins!

WHAT COLOR IS YOUR BELT?

The color of your belt shows how much tae kwon do you know.

The colors of the belts are a little different from place to place, but usually they are like this:

Beginning belts:
white
gold
orange

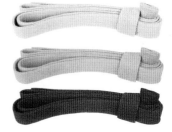

Intermediate belts:
green
purple
blue

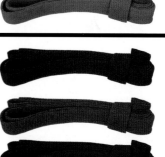

Advanced belts:
red
brown
black

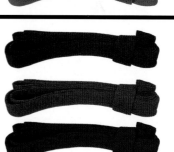

YOUR NEW WORDS

block (blok) a move to protect oneself from a punch or kick

bow (bou) to bend low to show respect

gi (gee) a loose-fitting uniform worn in tae kwon do

instructor (in-**struhk**-tuhr) someone who teaches others

kick (kik) to strike out with your foot

medal (**med**-uhl) a piece of metal shaped like a coin or star given to someone who won a sporting event

spar (spar) to fight while trying not to hurt the other person

FOUR
TAE KWON DO KICKS

Flying Side Kick

Roundhouse Kick

Spin Kick

Standing Side Kick

INDEX

FIND OUT MORE

Book:

Pierce, Terry, and Todd Bonita (illustrator). *Tae Kwon Do!* New York: Random House, 2006.

Website:

Scholastic Kids: The Black Belt Club
http://www.scholastic.com/blackbeltclub/

MEET THE AUTHOR

Laine Falk is a writer and Scholastic editor. She lives in Brooklyn, New York, with her family.